Discipleship: Following the Master

Participant's Guide

Terry Tieman

For more information, please contact
Transforming Churches Network
1160 Vickery Lane, Suite 1, Cordova, TN 38016
901-757-9700
www.tcnprocess.com
terry@transformingchurchesnetwork.org

TABLE OF CONTENTS

ACKNOWLEDGMENTS

Our sincere thanks to Steve Addison, a pioneer in discipleship movements around the world, and upon whose foundational work, we have built this study.

Steve Addison has been a life-long student of movements that renew and expand the Christian faith. Steve distills the characteristics of dynamic movements and makes them available to leaders committed to the multiplication of disciple-making churches.

Steve began his research into Christian movements in the late 1980s while planting a church in Melbourne, Australia.

He is the author of three books on movements:

- *Pioneering Movements: Leadership that Multiplies Disciples and Churches* (IVP 2015)
- *What Jesus Started: Joining the Movement, Changing the World* (IVP 2012)
- *Movements that Change the World: Five Keys to Spreading the Gospel* (IVP 2009)

Steve Addison's resources on movements and disciple-making can be found at **www.movements.net**.

Also, a huge shout-out and sincere thanks to the passionate people of Immanuel Lutheran Church in Memphis, Tennessee. You are truly the best for allowing us to test and experiment with the ideas contained in this study. As a living laboratory of disciples, you are demonstrating every day what it means to be disciples, following the Master. I can't think of any place or any church that I would rather be than Immanuel, Memphis!

A special thanks goes to Senior Pastor, Will Miller and Associate Pastor, Greg Prauner who have shown exceptional leadership in equipping, modeling, training, supporting, and discipling the saints at Immanuel. Your insights, critical thinking, and piloting of this discipleship process are not only making a huge kingdom difference in your own community, but by God's grace and power, are beginning to penetrate the darkness with light in other communities as well. Your courage, commitment, and friendship have been a huge inspiration for me and have helped see this training go from a seminal idea to a real plan of action.

Finally, my sincerest thanks and heartfelt gratitude to my mentor, colleague and friend, Dwight Marable, whose heart and passion for reaching lost people around the world continues to motivate me (and many others) to keep working, "as long as it is day" (John 9:4), so that as many people as possible may spend eternity with Jesus in heaven.

ᵓart 1: Reaching

ʝo...make disciples!

esus (Matthew 28:19)

esus started a grassroots Gospel movement that shook the world 2,000 ears ago and continues to grow like a tsunami in many parts of the world ɔday! But not so much here in North America... Why? Could it be because ve are overlooking the simple, but profound, kingdom principles that Jesus aught his first disciples?

he principles Jesus presented constitute the basic job description for naking and multiplying disciples in fulfillment of his Great Commission... nd they still work today! In this section, we are going to learn how to apply he methods that Jesus taught and modeled and start **REACHING OUT** to ɔst and unreached people, just as Jesus did!

ᑕome, follow me and I'll show you how to fish or people.

esus (Mark 1:17, CEB)

n many countries, if you examine a coin you will find that on one side depicts he head of an existing or former ruler. Jesus is our Ruler; he is our King. n Mark 1:17 he commands his first disciples to follow him. A follower is omeone who has pledged loyalty to him as their king.

here are two sides to every coin. On one side of the discipleship coin, we ecognize Jesus as our King. We obey him. On the other side of the coin, he ɔromises in Mark 1:17 to teach us how to fish for people. Fishing for people s the job of every disciple. You can't split a coin. You can't separate following esus from fishing for people. Nor can you be a faithful disciple without ɔeing serious about "going and making disciples" of others.

ᵓart 1 of this study shows us how to find and **REACH** more people who vant to follow Jesus.

Session 1

Following the Master

Objective: To grow in understanding of, passion for, and skills in making and reproducing disciples, like Jesus did.

Discovery Activity

Question #1: Who was your role model and why did you choose this person?

Question #2: Why do we try to be like other people? What is the purpose of role models?

Question #3: What's easier? Giving directions to your house, drawing a map, or just asking the person to follow you home? Why?

Learning Activity

What is a Disciple?

- ✓ A follower of Jesus; one who trusts in Jesus as Savior, takes up His teachings and lifestyle and teaches others how to do the same.
- ✓ Everything we are and do has discipleship in mind. *Matthew 28:19*

What do these passages have to say about how Jesus went about the task of making disciples? What do they say about the role Jesus' followers have in making new disciples?

Passage	Principles of Discipleship
ohn 1:35-42	
1atthew 16:24-25	
uke 11:1-2	
1atthew 11:28-30	
1ark 1:35-38	
lehemiah 1:1-4	

Practice Activity

raining Model

- ✓ Immediate Training
- ✓ I do it and you watch
- ✓ We do it together
- ✓ You do it and I watch
- ✓ Repeat...with a new disciple

esus' Final Words

Vhat did Jesus command his followers to do?

'et 98% of Christians don't share their faith. Why do you think that is?

Then Jesus came to them and said, "All authority in heaven and on earth has been given to me. Therefore go and make disciples of all nations, baptizing them in the name of the Father and of the Son and of the Holy Spirit, and teaching them to obey everything I have commanded you. And surely I am with you always, to the very end of the age." Matthew 28:18-20	MATTHEW 28:18-20 98% JESUS: "GO...MAKE DISCIPLES" -> DON'T 1. Why? 2. Who? 3. What? 4. How?

Over the next several weeks, we're going to answer 4 Questions that will help us become more effective in following the Master's command to make disciples.

If we can answer these four questions we'll be well on the way to obeying what Jesus commanded.

1.**Why** make disciples?

2.**Who** do you reach?

3.**What** do you say?

4.**How** do you ask for a response?

Application Activity

How willing are you to follow Jesus? How willing are you to help others follow Jesus? What struggles do you envision you will have in living out your faith.

Write a statement of your commitment to following Jesus below and share it with a partner. (This is not to make people feel guilty but to encourage them toward growth in their journey of following Jesus.) Then pray together that God would help you to become more committed to following Jesus.

Session 2

Why Make Disciples?

Objective: To have a clear understanding of why we should be involved in the disciple making process and to appreciate our identity as new people in Christ.

Learning Activity

Simon Says

1. What if the game was ***Jesus Says*** instead of ***Simon Says***? How well would you be doing?

2. Examine some of the things that Jesus says.

3. Is it really possible for us to do all of these things? Why or why not?

Passage	Command(s)
1. Mark 1:14-15	
2. Matthew 28:19	
3. Matthew 28:19	
4. Matthew 6:9	
5. Matthew 22:37-39	
6. Luke 22:19-20	
7. Luke 6:38	

Vhy?

Therefore, if anyone is in Christ, the new creation has come: The old has gone, the new is here!

All this is from God, who reconciled us to himself through Christ and gave us the ministry of reconciliation: that God was reconciling the world to himself in Christ, not counting people's sins against them.

And he has committed to us the message of reconciliation. We are therefore Christ's ambassadors, as though God were making his appeal through us. We implore you on Christ's behalf: Be reconciled to God. God made him who had no sin to be sin for us, so that in him we might become the righteousness of God.

2 Corinthians 5:17-21 ERV

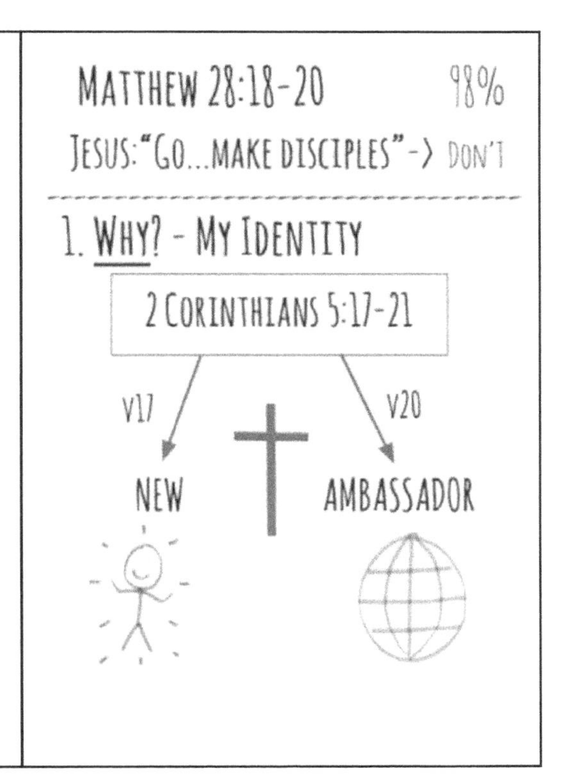

iscovery

Vhat words describe our new identity? (Answers are underlined in ne passage above.)

. New creation (v. 17) =

. Reconciled (v. 18) =

. Ambassador (v. 20) =

. Righteousness of God (v. 21) =

low did this happen?
he Great Exchange (Reversal) =

What does it mean to be Christ's ambassador?

1. What is our ministry? (v. 18)
2. What is our message (v. 21)

Practice Activity

Instructions: Pair up and practice explaining 2 Cor. 5:17-21, while drawing the illustrations. One person is the believer and the other is the seeker. After the first person has shared, have the second person reflect on what was done well and what needs to be improved. Then switch.

1. Was this easier or more difficult than you expected? Why?

2. What do you need to improve?

3. With whom could you practice this week?

Application Activity

Practice explaining and illustrating 2 Cor. 5:17-21 at least once a day this next week. Write the names of people you think you could share this with this week. Try to include a variety of people, including:

1. A member of this class =

2. Your spouse or another family member =

3. A friend =

4. A neighbor =

5. A stranger =

Session 3

Who Do You Reach?

Objective: To develop our own Relationship Map and begin praying for and thinking about ways to share the Gospel with people in our circle of influence who need to know Jesus.

Learning Activity

Who?

Then, leaving her water jar, the woman went back to the town and said to the people, "Come, see a man who told me everything I ever did. Could this be the Messiah?" They came out of the town and made their way toward him. John 4:28-30	

1. To whom does the woman go?

2. What does she say to them?

3. How soon after meeting Jesus does she do this?

4. What's the result?

'our Relationship Map

. Write your name and put a circle around it.

. Who do you know who is far from God? Think of friends, neighbors, work-mates, and family.

. Add the names of the people you know who are far from God.

. Identify the individuals and groups they know who are far from God. Jesus prayed for the people who would believe through his disciples (John 17:20).

Person of Peace

'he Woman at the Well is a God-prepared person or "person of eace" (Luke 10:1-10).

person of peace receives the:

Messenger = Invites you in or is hospitable

Message = Interested in hearing what you have to share

Mission = Is willing to share your message with people in his/her circle of influence

łow can you be a person of peace to the people in your world?

Where might you find persons of peace in your neighborhood? Community?

Application Activity

Pair up and pray through your Relationship Map with a partner. Ask your partner to pray for you and hold you accountable for praying fo the people on your list throughout the week. Put your Relationship Map somewhere you will see it often during the week, such as in you bible, on your bathroom mirror or on your refrigerator. Pray everyday for the people on your list.

Session 4

What Do You Say? (Your Story)

Objective: To become proficient at sharing the Gospel message by learning to share our own story of how Jesus changed our life.

Accountability Activity

Review the two questions of Why and Who using the folded piece of paper and illustrations from the previous sessions.

Learning Activity

What?

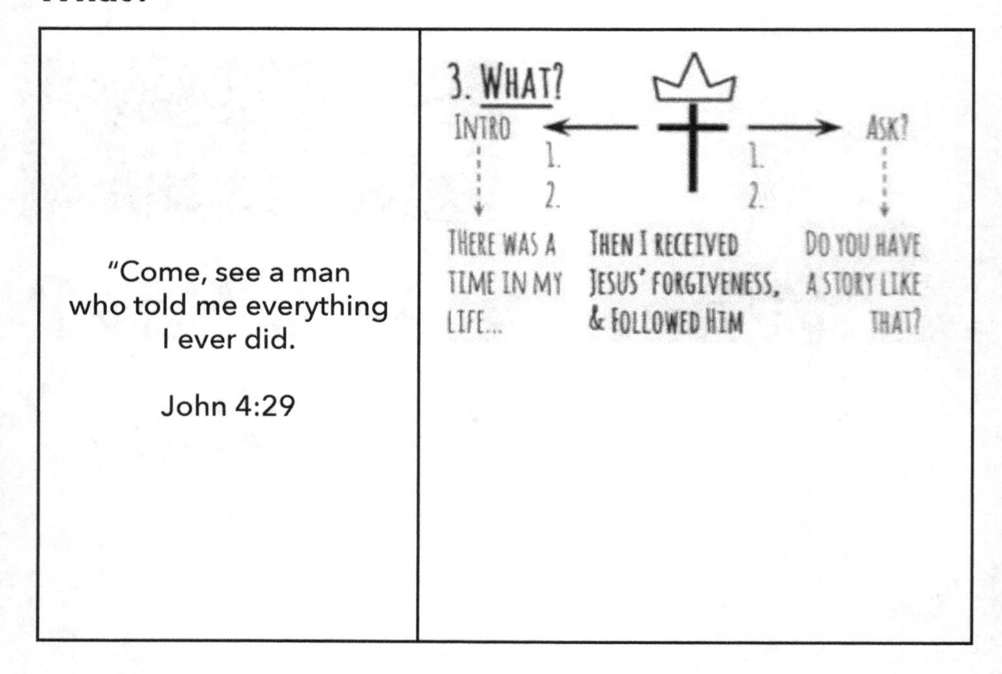

If people have a hard time relating to this exercise, have them reflect on this question: "What are some difficulties or challenges that God has helped you face that could serve as a connecting point with a non-believer?"

'our story

ike the Woman at the Well, we need to learn to share our story. ere is an outline you can use.

NTRODUCTION	LIFE BEFORE	MEETING JESUS	LIFE SINCE	QUESTION
		I took my faith seriously. God intervened in my life.		
'There was a :ime in my life…"	One or two statements describing your life distant from Christ	How you received forgiveness through his death and resurrection and began following Christ.	One or two statements describing your life following Christ.	Have you had an experience like that? Would you like to?

:xample:

'here was a time in my life when…

- *I had no hope left. I thought life wasn't worth living. I was far away from Jesus.*
- *I tried to solve all my problems myself.*
- *I thought God was far away and wasn't concerned about me or my problems.*
- *I took my relationship with Jesus for granted.*

'hen…

- *I received Jesus' forgiveness through his death for me. I was given the gift of faith by the Holy Spirit and began following Jesus as my king.*
- *I began to take my faith seriously and took everything to God in prayer.*
- *God became real to me and changed my life.*

Since then...

- *God has changed me from the inside out and given me a relationship with Him that will last forever.*
- *I have received an inner peace that helps me cope with even the most difficult situations.*
- *I know that there is nothing that God and I can't handle together.*
- *Have you had an experience like that?*

Your story in 30 seconds . . .
(Use this page to write out your story.)

Practice Activity

Instructions: Pair up and practice sharing your story with a partner, while using your time line. Be sure and use the notes that you wrote out above. One person is the believer and the other is the seeker. After the first person has shared, have the second person reflect on what was done well and what needs to be improved. Then switch.

1. Was this easier or more difficult than you expected? Why?

2. What do you need to improve?

3. With whom could you practice this week?

Application Activity

Practice explaining and illustrating your story at least once a day this next week. Write the names of people you think you could share this with this week. Try to include a variety of people, including:

1. A member of this class =
2. Your spouse or another family member =
3. A friend =
4. A neighbor =
5. A stranger =

Part 2: Responding

The Lord added to their number daily those who were being saved.

The Apostle Luke (Acts 2:47)

n Part 1 of this study, we have presented what it means to be a disciple or follower of Jesus, why it's important for us to "go and make disciples," who we should reach out to, and what we should ay, all in hopes that "people would be saved and come to the nowledge of the truth."

And yet, in reality many of us have yet to experience "making" ven one disciple. Certainly, very few have experienced the kind of xplosive kingdom growth outlined in the Book of Acts. But let us not be discouraged! Our great and awesome God has promised harvest when we liberally plant the seed of the Word of God Matthew 13:3-23)! The only question is the size of the harvest. Will it be "a hundred, sixty or thirty times what was sown"?

Thus, in Part 2, we are going to examine how to **RESPOND** to the 3 basic **RESPONSES** that people may give to the Gospel. What can we do to be faithful and effective seed sowers?

Many of the Samaritans from that town believed in him because of he woman's testimony.

The Apostle John (John 4:39)

If you have ever driven a car, you know what the signals above mean Of course, red means stop, yellow means caution (except in the city where I live, it means "speed up" or "don't stop or you will get rear-ended"), and green means go. Not heeding those signals, could result in getting a ticket or even having an accident.

In much the same way, when we share the Gospel with someone, the will give us some kind of signal as to how to proceed. Basically, those **RESPONSES**, can be divided into 3 categories: I'm not interested (re light) , I am interested but not ready (yellow light), or I am ready to move forward (green light). In this section of the study, we are going to be looking at practical ways to **RESPOND** to these **RESPONSES**!

Ready, set, go!

Session 5

The Great Commission Bridge

Objective: To examine the 3 responses that people may have to the Gospel and how to help a new disciple GO from their initial confession of faith to GOING and making disciples of others.

Learning Activity

Red Light/Green Light

1. *Red light – I'm not interested*

    - Smile and move on.
    - Read Luke 10:10-11

2. *Yellow light – I'm not ready*

    - Offer to meet again and discuss some stories about Jesus using the Seeker Series (see www.tcnprocess.com) or a portion of Scriptures, like the Gospel of Luke.
    - Give them resource such as a Project Connect booklet (www.lhm.org/projectconnect/booklets.asp) or TrueLife card (www.truelife.org) and ask them to view some of the videos.
    - Invite them to attend an Interest Group, Bible study or worship service at your church.
    - Make an appointment to meet again.

3. *Green light – I'm ready*

    - Ask them to tell you in their own words what they understood of the 3 Circles or Your Story.
    - Ask them if they believe what you shared with them about Jesus is true. Have them say what they believe in their own words.
    - Ask them if there is anything that is keeping them from receiving God's forgiveness and being Jesus' disciple.
    - Cross The Great Commission Bridge (See page 30.)

How?

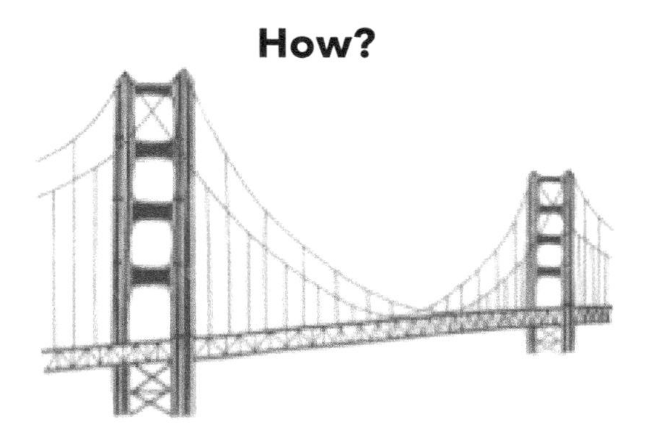

	HOW?
Then Jesus came to them and said, "All authority in heaven and on earth has been given to me. Therefore go and make disciples of all nations, baptizing them in the name of the Father and of the Son and of the Holy Spirit, and teaching them to obey everything I have commanded you. And surely I am with you always, to the very end of the age." Matthew 28:18-20	1. All Authority 2. Go & Make Disciples of All Nations 3. Baptizing 4. Teach & Obey 5. Always with you

he Great Commission Bridge

. Share Your Story or the 3 Circles.

2. Ask the Question: Is there anything that is keeping you from receiving God's forgiveness and being Jesus' disciple?

3. Cross the Great Commission Bridge

1) All authority in heaven and on earth has been given to me. (v. 18)

- What does this mean?

- Are you willing to have Jesus' be your king over everything in your life?

2) Therefore, go and make disciples of all nations, (v. 19)
- This is what we are doing right now.
- What is a disciple?
- Do you want to become like Jesus?
- Are you willing to follow Him?
- Would you like to meet on a regular basis to find out how to do that?
- Is there anyone else you know that you think might like to join you?
- Help them fill out their Relationship Map. (See Session 3.)
- Set a time to meet again within1-2 days and begin The Discipleship Journey. (See Session 7.)

3) Baptizing them in the name of the Father and of the Son and of the Holy Spirit, and (v. 19)
- What is baptism? (Baptism is applying water in the name of God.)
- What happens in baptism? (We receive the forgiveness of sins won for us on the cross by Jesus and the Holy Spirit gives us the gifts of faith and eternal life.)
- Are you willing to be baptized? When? (Set a date as soon as possible, when family and friends can attend.)

4) Teaching them to obey everything I have commanded you. (v. 20)
- When we meet together, we are going to teach you how to obey and follow Jesus.
- You will begin to understand what it means to be a disciple of Jesus and enjoy the blessings that come from following Him.

5) And surely I am with you always, to the very end of the age. (v. 20)
- Jesus promises to be with you throughout your entire life.

4. Summarize Commitments: You want to...

1) Receive Christ's forgiveness that He won for you through His life, death, and resurrection.

2) Be Jesus' disciple and follow Him.

3) Be baptized.

4) Learn to obey His teachings.

5) Understand He is always with you.

5. Confess in Your Own Words

- Read Romans 10:9
- Pray together
- Confirm when you will meet again to begin The Discipleship Journey.

Practice Activity

Instructions: Pair up and practice the Great Commission Bridge with a partner. One person is the believer and the other is the seeker. After the first person has shared, have the second person reflect on what was done well and what needs to be improved. Then switch. If there is time, do it again, beginning with Sharing Your Story or 3 Circles and then segueing to the Great Commission Bridge.

Debrief as a large group.

1. Was this easier or more difficult than you expected? Why?

2. What do you need to improve?

3. With whom could you practice this week?

Application Activity

Practice the Great Commission Bridge once a day this next week. Write the names of people you think you could share this with this week. Try to include a variety of people, including:

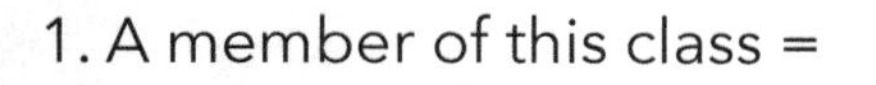

1. A member of this class =

2. Your spouse or another family member =

3. A friend =

4. A neighbor =

5. A stranger =

Session 6

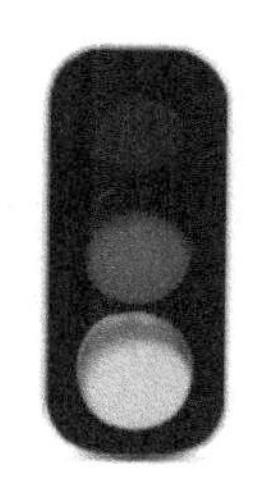

The Discipleship Journey

Objective: To introduce a one-on-one Discipleship process entitled, "The Discipleship Journey."

Session 1 – Assurance of Salvation

These note boxes contain important information. Be sure to read each "NOTE" out loud during your time together.

INTRODUCTION: This discipleship training is to be done either one-on-one or in small groups where one person is discipling the other(s).

☐ BEGIN BY PRAYING TOGETHER

☐ LIST A HIGHLIGHT FROM LAST WEEK & CHALLENGE YOU ARE FACING

Highlight	Challenge
______________________________	______________________________
______________________________	______________________________

☐ WHAT IS YOUR SPIRITUAL CONDITION?

Romans 10:9 (NLT) If you confess with your mouth that Jesus is Lord and believe in your heart that God raised him from the dead you will be saved.

Have you confessed Jesus as your Lord?

☐ Yes ☐ No ☐ I'm Not Sure

Do you believe in your heart God raised Him from the dead?

☐ Yes ☐ No ☐ I'm Not Sure

If you answered "yes" to both questions, what does this passage say is your condition?

] READ AND DISCUSS EACH SCRIPTURE BELOW:

The Purpose of this Session is to help you understand what happened to you when you confessed your faith in Jesus. Here are Bible verses to help you understand and be certain of your new relationship in Christ.

) ***John 1:12 (NKJV) But as many as received Him, to them He gave the right to become children of God, to those who believe in His name.***

What makes you a child of God?

2) ***Acts 16:31 (NKJV) So they said, "Believe on the Lord Jesus Christ, and you will be saved, you and your household."***
When the Bible says saved, what are you saved from?

3) ***Romans 3:28 (NIV84) For we maintain that a man is justified by faith apart from observing the law.***

What causes you to be "justified?" (Justified means that you are no longer under the penalty of your sin.)

4) ***Romans 4:5 (NLT) But people are counted as righteous, not because of their work, but because of their faith in God who forgives sinners.***

What causes you to be counted as righteous before God?

5) ***Ephesians 2:8-9 (NIV84) For it is by grace you have been saved, through faith—and this not from yourselves, it is the gift of God—not by works, so that no one can boast.***

What can't you do because you have been saved by grace through faith?

6) ***John 5:24 (NIV84) "I tell you the truth, whoever hears my word and believes him who sent me has eternal life and will not be condemned; he has crossed over from death to life."***

As a believer, what can never happen to you?

7) ***John 10:27-29 (NLT) "My sheep listen to my voice; I know them, and they follow me. 28 I give them eternal life, and they will never perish. No one can snatch them away from me, 29 for my Father has given them to me, and he is more powerful than anyone else. No one can snatch them from the Father's hand."***

How secure are you in God's hand?

8) Romans 8:38–39 (NLT) And I am convinced that nothing can ever separate us from God's love. Neither death nor life, neither angels nor demons, neither our fears for today nor our worries about tomorrow—not even the powers of hell can separate us from God's love. 39 No power in the sky above or in the earth below—indeed, nothing in all creation will ever be able to separate us from the love of God that is revealed in Christ Jesus our Lord.

From what can you never be separated?

9) 1 John 5:11–13 (NIV84) And this is the testimony: God has given us eternal life, and this life is in his Son. 12 He who has the Son has life; he who does not have the Son of God does not have life. 13 I write these things to you who believe in the name of the Son of God so that you may know that you have eternal life.

Do you know whether or not you have eternal life?
Is your salvation secure?

☐ Yes ☐ No ☐ I'm Not Sure

ASSIGNMENT FOR NEXT TIME:

1. READ: Begin reading the Gospel of John before the next session.

Why should you start with the Gospel of John? Because of the purpose of the Gospel of John:

John 20:30–31 (NLT) The disciples saw Jesus do many other miraculous signs in addition to the ones recorded in this book. But these are written so that you may continue to believe that Jesus is the Messiah, the Son of God, and that by believing in him you will have life by the power of his name.

Read one chapter per day for the purpose of getting to know Jesus better and growing in your faith.

2. MEMORIZE this Bible verse:
   Romans 10:9 (NLT) If you confess with your mouth that Jesus is Lord and believe in your heart that God raised him from the dead, you will be saved.

☐ CLOSE IN PRAYER TOGETHER

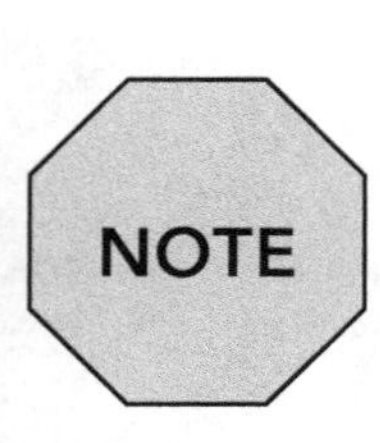

There are 8 sessions in *The Discipleship Journey* training series. The other sessions are: Baptism, Prayer, Bible Study & Devotions, Your Faith Story, God's Story—The Bridge, Church: Christian Community, and Practice Being the Church. The last session will lead into a Discovery Bible Study called *Thru the Bible*, which we will talk about later.

Debrief as a large group.

1. What went well?

2. What was difficult?

3. What do you need to improve?

4. What is the benefit of this process?

5. Whom could you invite to join you in The Discipleship Journey this week?

Application Activity

Continue praying for the people from your Relationship Map. Resolve to share Your Story or the 3 Circles with at least one person from that list this week. If they give you a Green Light, share the Great Commission Bridge with them and invite them to begin *The Discipleship Journey*.

Session 7

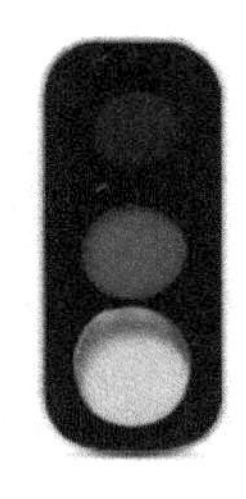

Discovery Bible Study

Objective: To learn how to form and lead a gathering of disciples, using a three-part format called a Discovery Bible Study.

Discovery Bible Study

A disciple is someone who is following Jesus and learning how to fish for people. Here is a simple way of gathering with other disciples to learn how to follow and fish in three parts.

First Third: Look back

1. Care

- Ask, "How are you doing? What are you thankful for? How are you struggling?
- Pray for any needs in the group.
- Be careful not to let this segment dominate your time together.

2. Worship

- Find a simple, relevant way to worship God.
- For example: read a passage of the Bible or a Psalm and respond to God in prayer; or sing songs of worship, using a CD or guitar, if someone in your group can play.

3. Accountability

Follow

- How did you obey the lesson from last time?
- How are you growing in your relationship with Jesus? With loving one another?
- How has God been speaking to you lately and how have you responded? Be specific.

Fish

- Did you pray with anyone who was in need?
- Did you spend time with anyone from your Relationship Map?
- Did you find a person of peace?
- Did you share Your Story or the 3 Circles?

Did you share the Great Commission Bridge with anyone?

Did you invite anyone to this Discovery Bible Study?

. Casting vision for reaching lost people and making disciples.

Share an encouraging challenge to reach people far from God.

For example, tell what Matthew 28:18-20 means to you and what you believe God is going to do through this group and your church.

econd Third: Look up

. New lesson

ead the Bible story or passage.

Without looking at the text, retell the passage in your own words.

What does the passage teach us about God?

What does it teach us about people?

How will you apply this passage to your own life?

Is there a command to obey or an example to follow?

xample: Jesus Teaching His Disciples to Pray (Matthew 6:5-15)

Read the story.

Retell the passage in your own words.

What does the passage teach us about God?

What does the story teach us about people?

How can we apply this to our own lives?

Is there a command to obey or an example to follow?

inal Third: Look forward

. Practice

Practice or retell the new lesson you have learned.

• Write out Matthew 6:5-15 in your own words.

7. Set goals and pray

• What do you need to do this week to obey what you've learned?

• Who could you share this passage with?

• Pray for your group, the lost, and for your goals that you have set.

Practice Activity

Read over the outline below, then see how much of it you can write out from memory.

Look back

1. **Mutual care**: How are you doing?
2. **Worship**: Praising God in a simple, relevant way.
3. **Accountability**
   - *Follow*: How did you obey the lesson from last time?
   - *Fish*: Did you pray with anyone who was in need?
   - Did you share Your Story or the 3 Circles?
   - Did you share the Great Commission Bridge?
   - Did you find a person of peace?
4. **Casting vision** for reaching lost people and making disciples.

Look up

5. **New lesson**:

Learn:

1. Retell the passage in your own words.
2. What did we learn about Jesus, others?

Obey:

1. How will you apply this to your own life or help someone else apply it to their life?
2. Is there a command to obey or an example to follow?

Look forward

6. **Practice** the lesson unti everyone is confident and competent to appl the learning.
7. **Set goals and pray**: Goals for personal growth, sharing the gospel, and training or inviting others.

Application Activity

Continue praying for the people from your Relationship Map. Resolve to share Your Story or the 3 Circles with at least one person from that list this week. If they give you a Green Light, share the Great Commission Bridge with them and invite them to begin The Discipleship Journey.

Session 8

Where Do We Go From Here?

Objective: To outline various steps individuals, the class, and the church can take to move forward in the disciple making process as they continue to follow the Master.

Learning Activity

Wise or Foolish?

Therefore everyone who hears these words of mine and puts them into practice is like a wise man who built his house on the rock. The rain came down, the streams rose, and the winds blew and beat against that house; yet it did not fall, because it had its foundation on the rock. But everyone who hears these words and does not put them into practice is like a foolish man who built his house on sand. The rain came down, the streams rose, and the winds blew and beat against that house and it fell with a great crash.

Matthew 7:24-26

Discovery

What are the similarities between the two men in Jesus parable?

What are the differences?

Which are you most like? Why?

iscussion

uestion #1: What was easy to learn and implement in this study? Vhat was difficult? Which part of Jesus' call to discipleship has been ne hardest for you to follow? Why?

uestion #2: What did you like from this study? What didn't you ke? Why?

uestion #3: Whose lives have you impacted as a result of this aining? How? Which parts of the training have you implemented?

- ☐ Relationship Map
- ☐ Your Story
- ☐ 3 Circles
- ☐ Great Commission Bridge
- ☐ The Discipleship Journey

uestion #4: How have you been changed as a result of this training?

Application Activity

Question #1: Who do you have on your heart right now that really needs to hear the Gospel and know about Jesus life, death, and resurrection personally?

Question #2: Would you be willing to be used by God to be the one to share that saving message with your friend? Would you be willing to go with someone else to support them in doing the same?

Question #3: What help and support do you need right now to follow Jesus and be a disciple maker? From a partner? From your pastor? From your church?

Then pray together that God would help you to follow Jesus and fish for people!

Appendix

What Do You Say? (3 Circles)

Objective: To learn a new, simple, and non-threatening way to communicate the Gospel message using the 3 Circles approach.

Learning Activity

What?

The jailer called for lights, rushed in and fell trembling before Paul and Silas. He then brought them out and asked, "Sirs, what must I do to be saved?" They replied, "Believe in the Lord Jesus and you will be saved–you and your household." Then they spoke the word of the Lord to him and to all the others in his house. At that hour of the night the jailer took them and washed their wounds; then immediately he and all his family were baptized. The jailer brought them into his house and set a meal before them; he was filled with joy because he had come to believe in God–he and his whole family. Acts16:29-34	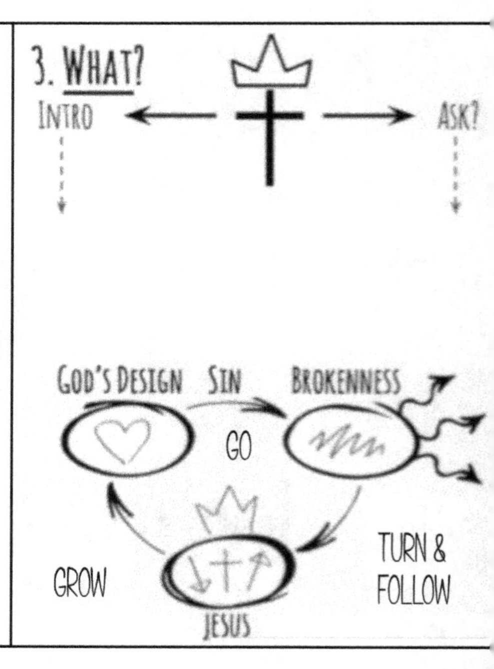

1. How did Paul and Silas respond to the jailer's question: "what mus I do to be saved?"

2. What does it mean to "believe in the Lord Jesus and you will be saved"? (Romans 10:9-10) What do you think Paul and Silas said when they "spoke the word of the Lord" to the jailer and his household?

3. How did the jailer respond to this message?

4. What should you say to those who want to know (or need to know) how to be saved?

'he 3 Circles

ou need a simple way of communicating the gospel and asking for response.

. Use a bridge:

How can I pray for you?
Do you feel near or far from God?
Could I share with you how you could be near to God (or how I became near to God)?

. Draw and explain the 3 Circles

Vatch the presentation at: **https://youtu.be/NYU-a2wlbxc** or **ttps://youtu.be/V7mURm-8cOI**

. Ask the 3 Questions

Which circle best describes your life right now?
Listen, then ask, "Where would you like to be?"
Is there anything stopping you from responding to Jesus now?
(Instructions on where to go from here will be given in the next session.)

Practice Activity

nstructions: Pair up and practice the 3 Circles with a partner, while rawing the illustrations. One person is the believer and the other is ne seeker. After the first person has shared, have the second person eflect on what was done well and what needs to be improved. Then witch. Repeat.

)ebrief as a large group.

. Was this easier or more difficult than you expected? Why?

. What do you need to improve?

. With whom could you practice this week?

Application Activity

Practice the 3 Circles once a day this next week. Write the names of people you think you could share this with this week. Try to include a variety of people, including:

1. A member of this class =

2. Your spouse or another family member =

3. A friend =

4. A neighbor =

5. A stranger =

More Discipleship Resources from TCN

The Discipleship Journey

A one-on-one discipleship training series designed to be used following *Making Disciples: Following the Master* or whenever a new believer has confessed faith in Christ.

Bible Studies/ Training Series

Motivation for Mission: Embracing God's Vision for Your Community
Catching Vision: Seeing a New Future for Your Church
Natural Evangelism: Sharing the Gospel in Ways that are Truly Good
Prayer: The First Step in Reaching Your Community
People of Passion: Activities for Opening Doors to Your Community
Skill Builders: Leadership Tools for Opening Doors to Your Community

Hinges

Identify the 8 key factors, called Hinges, that can help shift inwardly-focused congregations into churches that open their doors to the community. Resources include 1) the *Hinges* book, which describes the 8 Hinge factors, complete with a Discussion Guide and Best Practices, 2) the *Hinge Factors Assessment Survey,* an electronic survey that measures how well a congregation and its Pastor are doing in each of the 8 Hinge Factors, and 3) *Hinge Events,* workshops that help churches discover creative ways to open new doors to their community.

Consultations/ Processes

Designed to identify specific issues and give recommendations to the congregation with regard to its ability to reach out to lost and unreached individuals in its community. Choose *The 19:10 Project.* (weekend consultation) or *Seasons of Discovery* (2-year process).

Coaching

Trained coaches support pastors through problem solving, empowering their members and working on discipleship processes in their church.

CPSIA information can be obtained
at www.ICGtesting.com
Printed in the USA
LVHW04s2125240918
591250LV00006B/24/P